Date _____ Address _____

Name _____

School _____

Grade/Form/Year and Age _____

When I started playing soccer _____

Who taught me soccer first _____

Now I play at _____

My coach is _____

Who assist coach _____

My coach calls me _____

Why I like my coach _____

_____

_____

_____

My coach often tells me _____

_____

_____

_____

My coach often tells me _____

_____

_____

_____

Why I like playing soccer _____

_____

_____

_____

My goal is _____

_____

_____

_____

My favorite teams:
1. _____
2. _____
3. _____

My favorite players:
(1.) _____
(2.) _____
(3.) _____

Three things I admire most about each favorite player

(1.) -- _____

-- _____

-- _____

(2.) -- _____

-- _____

-- _____

(3.) -- _____

-- _____

_____

The interesting things about soccer _____

_____

_____

_____

The funny thing ever happened to me playing soccer_____

_____

_____

_____

The bad/weird thing ever happened to me playing soccer _____

_____

_____

_____

PRE-SEASON PRACTICE

From Monday _____ to Friday _____ How many times _____
Date   Date

1st practice was: Very easy ☐ Easy ☐ Average ☐ Hard ☐ Very hard ☐

2nd practice was: Very easy ☐ Easy ☐ Average ☐ Hard ☐ Very hard ☐

3rd practice was: Very easy ☐ Easy ☐ Average ☐ Hard ☐ Very hard ☐

1st practice: ☺ 😐 ☹ 2nd practice: ☺ 😐 ☹ 3rd practice: ☺ 😐 ☹

Coach focused on _____
_____
_____
_____

I focused on _____
_____
_____
_____

What I'v learnt _____
_____
_____

My weaknesses/strengths _____
_____
_____

Coach advice _____
_____
_____
_____

Additional notes _____
_____
_____

PRE-SEASON PRACTICE

From Monday _____ to Friday _____ How many times _____
Date   Date

1st practice was: Very easy ☐ Easy ☐ Average ☐ Hard ☐ Very hard ☐
2nd practice was: Very easy ☐ Easy ☐ Average ☐ Hard ☐ Very hard ☐
3rd practice was: Very easy ☐ Easy ☐ Average ☐ Hard ☐ Very hard ☐

1st practice: 🙂 😐 🙁   2nd practice: 🙂 😐 🙁   3rd practice: 🙂 😐 🙁

Coach focused on
_____
_____
_____
_____

I focused on
_____
_____
_____

What I'v learnt
_____
_____
_____

My weaknesses/strengths
_____
_____
_____

Coach advice
_____
_____
_____

Additional notes
_____
_____

PRE-SEASON PRACTICE

From Monday _____ to Friday _____ How many times _____
Date   Date

1st practice was: Very easy ☐ Easy ☐ Average ☐ Hard ☐ Very hard ☐
2nd practice was: Very easy ☐ Easy ☐ Average ☐ Hard ☐ Very hard ☐
3rd practice was: Very easy ☐ Easy ☐ Average ☐ Hard ☐ Very hard ☐

1st practice: ☺ 😐 ☹   2nd practice: ☺ 😐 ☹   3rd practice: ☺ 😐 ☹

Coach focused on
_____
_____
_____
_____

I focused on
_____
_____
_____

What I'v learnt
_____
_____
_____

My weaknesses/strengths
_____
_____

Coach advice
_____
_____
_____

Additional notes
_____
_____

PRE-SEASON PRACTICE

From Monday _____ to Friday _____ How many times _____
Date   Date

1st practice was: Very easy ☐ Easy ☐ Average ☐ Hard ☐ Very hard ☐

2nd practice was: Very easy ☐ Easy ☐ Average ☐ Hard ☐ Very hard ☐

3rd practice was: Very easy ☐ Easy ☐ Average ☐ Hard ☐ Very hard ☐

1st practice: 🙂 😐 🙁   2nd practice: 🙂 😐 🙁   3rd practice: 🙂 😐 🙁

Coach focused on
_____
_____
_____

I focused on
_____
_____
_____

What I'v learnt
_____
_____
_____

My weaknesses/strengths
_____
_____
_____

Coach advice
_____
_____
_____

Additional notes
_____
_____

PRACTICE

From Monday _____ to ⟨ Friday _____   How many times ___
          Date   Date
                 next game _____   How many times ___
                        Date

1st practice was: Very easy ☐   Easy ☐   Average ☐   Hard ☐   Very hard ☐

2nd practice was: Very easy ☐   Easy ☐   Average ☐   Hard ☐   Very hard ☐

3rd practice was: Very easy ☐   Easy ☐   Average ☐   Hard ☐   Very hard ☐

1st practice: ☺ 😐 ☹   2nd practice: ☺ 😐 ☹   3rd practice: ☺ 😐 ☹

Coach focused on
_____
_____
_____
_____

I focused on
_____
_____
_____

What I'v learnt
_____
_____
_____

My weaknesses/strengths
_____
_____
_____

Coach advice
_____
_____
_____

Additional notes
_____
_____

PRACTICE

From Monday _____ to ⟨ Friday _____ How many times ___
                        Date
                       ⟨ next game _____ How many times ___
                                     Date

1st practice was: Very easy ☐ Easy ☐ Average ☐ Hard ☐ Very hard ☐

2nd practice was: Very easy ☐ Easy ☐ Average ☐ Hard ☐ Very hard ☐

3rd practice was: Very easy ☐ Easy ☐ Average ☐ Hard ☐ Very hard ☐

1st practice: ☺ 😐 ☹   2nd practice: ☺ 😐 ☹   3rd practice: ☺ 😐 ☹

Coach focused on
_____
_____
_____

I focused on
_____
_____

What I'v learnt
_____
_____

My weaknesses/strengths
_____
_____

Coach advice
_____
_____
_____

Additional notes
_____
_____

PRACTICE

From Monday _____ to < Friday _____ How many times ___
                Date   Date
              to < next game _____ How many times ___
                                Date

1st practice was: Very easy ☐ Easy ☐ Average ☐ Hard ☐ Very hard ☐

2nd practice was: Very easy ☐ Easy ☐ Average ☐ Hard ☐ Very hard ☐

3rd practice was: Very easy ☐ Easy ☐ Average ☐ Hard ☐ Very hard ☐

1st practice: ☺ 😐 ☹   2nd practice: ☺ 😐 ☹   3rd practice: ☺ 😐 ☹

Coach focused on
_____
_____
_____

I focused on
_____
_____
_____

What I'v learnt
_____
_____
_____

My weaknesses/strengths
_____
_____

Coach advice
_____
_____
_____

Additional notes
_____
_____

PRACTICE

From Monday _____ to ⟨ Friday _____ How many times ___
$\qquad$ Date $\qquad$ Date
next game _____ How many times ___
Date

1st practice was: Very easy ☐ Easy ☐ Average ☐ Hard ☐ Very hard ☐

2nd practice was: Very easy ☐ Easy ☐ Average ☐ Hard ☐ Very hard ☐

3rd practice was: Very easy ☐ Easy ☐ Average ☐ Hard ☐ Very hard ☐

1st practice: ☺ 😐 ☹   2nd practice: ☺ 😐 ☹   3rd practice: ☺ 😐 ☹

Coach focused on
_____
_____
_____

I focused on
_____
_____
_____

What I'v learnt
_____
_____
_____

My weaknesses/strengths
_____
_____
_____

Coach advice
_____
_____
_____

Additional notes
_____
_____

PRACTICE

From Monday _____ to Friday _____ How many times ___
Date   Date
to next game _____ How many times ___
                Date

1ˢᵗ practice was: Very easy ☐ Easy ☐ Average ☐ Hard ☐ Very hard ☐
2ⁿᵈ practice was: Very easy ☐ Easy ☐ Average ☐ Hard ☐ Very hard ☐
3ʳᵈ practice was: Very easy ☐ Easy ☐ Average ☐ Hard ☐ Very hard ☐

1ˢᵗ practice: ☺ ☹ ☹ 2ⁿᵈ practice: ☺ ☹ ☹ 3ʳᵈ practice: ☺ ☹ ☹

Coach focused on
_____
_____
_____
_____

I focused on
_____
_____
_____
_____

What I'v learnt
_____
_____
_____

My weaknesses/strengths
_____
_____
_____

Coach advice
_____
_____
_____

Additional notes
_____
_____
_____

PRACTICE

From Monday _____ to < Friday _____ How many times ___
                Date   Date
                        next game _____ How many times ___
                                  Date

1st practice was: Very easy ☐ Easy ☐ Average ☐ Hard ☐ Very hard ☐
2nd practice was: Very easy ☐ Easy ☐ Average ☐ Hard ☐ Very hard ☐
3rd practice was: Very easy ☐ Easy ☐ Average ☐ Hard ☐ Very hard ☐

1st practice: ☺ 😐 ☹   2nd practice: ☺ 😐 ☹   3rd practice: ☺ 😐 ☹

Coach focused on
_____
_____
_____

I focused on
_____
_____
_____

What I'v learnt
_____
_____
_____

My weaknesses/strengths
_____
_____
_____

Coach advice
_____
_____
_____

Additional notes
_____
_____

PRACTICE

From Monday _____ to ⟨ Friday _____   How many times ___
Date   next game _____   How many times ___
Date   Date

1st practice was: Very easy ☐   Easy ☐   Average ☐   Hard ☐   Very hard ☐

2nd practice was: Very easy ☐   Easy ☐   Average ☐   Hard ☐   Very hard ☐

3rd practice was: Very easy ☐   Easy ☐   Average ☐   Hard ☐   Very hard ☐

1st practice: ☺ 😐 ☹   2nd practice: ☺ 😐 ☹   3rd practice: ☺ 😐 ☹

Coach focused on
_____
_____
_____
_____

I focused on
_____
_____
_____

What I'v learnt
_____
_____
_____

My weaknesses/strengths
_____
_____
_____

Coach advice
_____
_____
_____

Additional notes
_____
_____
_____

PRACTICE

From Monday _____ to ⟨ Friday _____ How many times ___
                          Date
                         next game _____ How many times ___
                                    Date

1st practice was: Very easy ☐ Easy ☐ Average ☐ Hard ☐ Very hard ☐
2nd practice was: Very easy ☐ Easy ☐ Average ☐ Hard ☐ Very hard ☐
3rd practice was: Very easy ☐ Easy ☐ Average ☐ Hard ☐ Very hard ☐

1st practice: 🙂 😐 🙁   2nd practice: 🙂 😐 🙁   3rd practice: 🙂 😐 🙁

Coach focused on
_____
_____
_____

I focused on
_____
_____
_____

What I'v learnt
_____
_____
_____

My weaknesses/strengths
_____
_____
_____

Coach advice
_____
_____
_____

Additional notes
_____
_____

PRACTICE

From Monday _____ to ⟨ Friday _____   How many times __
         Date   Date
                next game _____   How many times __
                     Date

1st practice was: Very easy ☐ Easy ☐ Average ☐ Hard ☐ Very hard ☐

2nd practice was: Very easy ☐ Easy ☐ Average ☐ Hard ☐ Very hard ☐

3rd practice was: Very easy ☐ Easy ☐ Average ☐ Hard ☐ Very hard ☐

1st practice: ☺ 😐 ☹ 2nd practice: ☺ 😐 ☹ 3rd practice: ☺ 😐 ☹

Coach focused on
_____
_____
_____

I focused on
_____
_____
_____

What I'v learnt
_____
_____
_____

My weaknesses/strengths
_____
_____
_____

Coach advice
_____
_____
_____

Additional notes
_____
_____

PRACTICE

From Monday _____ to < Friday _____ How many times ___
Date   next game _____ How many times ___
Date   Date

1st practice was: Very easy ☐ Easy ☐ Average ☐ Hard ☐ Very hard ☐

2nd practice was: Very easy ☐ Easy ☐ Average ☐ Hard ☐ Very hard ☐

3rd practice was: Very easy ☐ Easy ☐ Average ☐ Hard ☐ Very hard ☐

1st practice: ☺ 😐 ☹ 2nd practice: ☺ 😐 ☹ 3rd practice: ☺ 😐 ☹

Coach focused on
_____
_____
_____

I focused on
_____
_____
_____

What I'v learnt
_____
_____
_____

My weaknesses/strengths
_____
_____
_____

Coach advice
_____
_____
_____

Additional notes
_____
_____
_____

PRACTICE

From Monday _____ to Friday _____ How many times ___
                   Date   Date

next game _____ How many times ___
                   Date

1st practice was: Very easy ☐ Easy ☐ Average ☐ Hard ☐ Very hard ☐

2nd practice was: Very easy ☐ Easy ☐ Average ☐ Hard ☐ Very hard ☐

3rd practice was: Very easy ☐ Easy ☐ Average ☐ Hard ☐ Very hard ☐

1st practice: 🙂 😐 🙁 2nd practice: 🙂 😐 🙁 3rd practice: 🙂 😐 🙁

Coach focused on
_____
_____
_____
_____

I focused on
_____
_____
_____

What I'v learnt
_____
_____
_____

My weaknesses/strengths
_____
_____
_____

Coach advice
_____
_____
_____

Additional notes
_____
_____

PRACTICE

From Monday _____ to Friday _____ How many times ___
Date   next game _____ How many times ___
                                   Date

1st practice was: Very easy ☐ Easy ☐ Average ☐ Hard ☐ Very hard ☐
2nd practice was: Very easy ☐ Easy ☐ Average ☐ Hard ☐ Very hard ☐
3rd practice was: Very easy ☐ Easy ☐ Average ☐ Hard ☐ Very hard ☐

1st practice: 🙂 😐 🙁   2nd practice: 🙂 😐 🙁   3rd practice: 🙂 😐 🙁

Coach focused on
_____
_____
_____

I focused on
_____
_____
_____

What I'v learnt
_____
_____
_____

My weaknesses/strengths
_____
_____
_____

Coach advice
_____
_____
_____

Additional notes
_____
_____
_____

PRACTICE

From Monday _____ to ⟨ Friday _____ How many times ___
                        Date
                          next game _____ How many times ___
                                      Date

1st practice was: Very easy ☐ Easy ☐ Average ☐ Hard ☐ Very hard ☐
2nd practice was: Very easy ☐ Easy ☐ Average ☐ Hard ☐ Very hard ☐
3rd practice was: Very easy ☐ Easy ☐ Average ☐ Hard ☐ Very hard ☐

1st practice: 🙂 😐 🙁   2nd practice: 🙂 😐 🙁   3rd practice: 🙂 😐 🙁

Coach focused on _____
_____
_____
_____

I focused on _____
_____
_____

What I'v learnt _____
_____
_____

My weaknesses/strengths _____
_____
_____

Coach advice _____
_____
_____

Additional notes _____
_____
_____

PRACTICE

From Monday _____ to ⟨ Friday _____   How many times ___
           Date   next game _____   How many times ___
                                      Date   Date

1st practice was: Very easy ☐   Easy ☐   Average ☐   Hard ☐   Very hard ☐

2nd practice was: Very easy ☐   Easy ☐   Average ☐   Hard ☐   Very hard ☐

3rd practice was: Very easy ☐   Easy ☐   Average ☐   Hard ☐   Very hard ☐

1st practice: ☺ 😐 ☹   2nd practice: ☺ 😐 ☹   3rd practice: ☺ 😐 ☹

Coach focused on
_____
_____
_____

I focused on
_____
_____
_____

What I'v learnt
_____
_____
_____

My weaknesses/strengths
_____
_____
_____

Coach advice
_____
_____
_____

Additional notes
_____
_____

PRACTICE

From Monday _____ to < Friday _____ How many times ___
Date
next game _____ How many times ___
Date Date

1st practice was: Very easy ☐ Easy ☐ Average ☐ Hard ☐ Very hard ☐

2nd practice was: Very easy ☐ Easy ☐ Average ☐ Hard ☐ Very hard ☐

3rd practice was: Very easy ☐ Easy ☐ Average ☐ Hard ☐ Very hard ☐

1st practice: ☺ 😐 ☹   2nd practice: ☺ 😐 ☹   3rd practice: ☺ 😐 ☹

Coach focused on
_____
_____
_____

I focused on
_____
_____
_____

What I'v learnt
_____
_____
_____

My weaknesses/strengths
_____
_____
_____

Coach advice
_____
_____
_____

Additional notes
_____
_____

PRACTICE

From Monday _____ to < Friday _____ How many times ___
                             Date
                          next game _____ How many times ___
                                        Date

1st practice was: Very easy ☐ Easy ☐ Average ☐ Hard ☐ Very hard ☐

2nd practice was: Very easy ☐ Easy ☐ Average ☐ Hard ☐ Very hard ☐

3rd practice was: Very easy ☐ Easy ☐ Average ☐ Hard ☐ Very hard ☐

1st practice: 🙂 😐 🙁   2nd practice: 🙂 😐 🙁   3rd practice: 🙂 😐 🙁

Coach focused on
_____
_____
_____

I focused on
_____
_____
_____

What I'v learnt
_____
_____
_____

My weaknesses/strengths
_____
_____
_____

Coach advice
_____
_____
_____

Additional notes
_____
_____

PRACTICE

From Monday _____ to ⟨ Friday _____   How many times ___
           Date   next game _____   How many times ___
                              Date

1st practice was: Very easy ☐   Easy ☐   Average ☐   Hard ☐   Very hard ☐

2nd practice was: Very easy ☐   Easy ☐   Average ☐   Hard ☐   Very hard ☐

3rd practice was: Very easy ☐   Easy ☐   Average ☐   Hard ☐   Very hard ☐

1st practice: ☺ 😐 ☹   2nd practice: ☺ 😐 ☹   3rd practice: ☺ 😐 ☹

Coach focused on
_____
_____
_____
_____

I focused on
_____
_____
_____

What I'v learnt
_____
_____
_____

My weaknesses/strengths
_____
_____
_____

Coach advice
_____
_____
_____

Additional notes
_____
_____
_____

PRACTICE

From Monday _____ to < Friday _____   How many times ___
          Date   next game _____   How many times ___
                               Date   Date

1st practice was: Very easy ☐ Easy ☐ Average ☐ Hard ☐ Very hard ☐

2nd practice was: Very easy ☐ Easy ☐ Average ☐ Hard ☐ Very hard ☐

3rd practice was: Very easy ☐ Easy ☐ Average ☐ Hard ☐ Very hard ☐

1st practice: ☺ 😐 ☹   2nd practice: ☺ 😐 ☹   3rd practice: ☺ 😐 ☹

Coach focused on _____
_____
_____
_____

I focused on _____
_____
_____

What I'v learnt _____
_____
_____

My weaknesses/strengths _____
_____
_____

Coach advice _____
_____
_____

Additional notes _____
_____
_____

PRACTICE

From Monday _____ to < Friday _____ How many times ___
                  Date   Date
          next game _____ How many times ___
                       Date

1st practice was: Very easy ☐ Easy ☐ Average ☐ Hard ☐ Very hard ☐
2nd practice was: Very easy ☐ Easy ☐ Average ☐ Hard ☐ Very hard ☐
3rd practice was: Very easy ☐ Easy ☐ Average ☐ Hard ☐ Very hard ☐

1st practice: 🙂 😐 🙁   2nd practice: 🙂 😐 🙁   3rd practice: 🙂 😐 🙁

Coach focused on _____
_____
_____
_____

I focused on _____
_____
_____

What I'v learnt _____
_____
_____

My weaknesses/strengths _____
_____
_____

Coach advice _____
_____
_____

Additional notes _____
_____
_____

PRACTICE

From Monday _____ to < Friday _____ How many times ___
Date   Date
next game _____ How many times ___
Date

1st practice was: Very easy ☐ Easy ☐ Average ☐ Hard ☐ Very hard ☐

2nd practice was: Very easy ☐ Easy ☐ Average ☐ Hard ☐ Very hard ☐

3rd practice was: Very easy ☐ Easy ☐ Average ☐ Hard ☐ Very hard ☐

1st practice: ☺ 😐 ☹ 2nd practice: ☺ 😐 ☹ 3rd practice: ☺ 😐 ☹

Coach focused on
_____
_____
_____

I focused on
_____
_____

What I'v learnt
_____
_____

My weaknesses/strengths
_____
_____

Coach advice
_____
_____
_____

Additional notes
_____
_____

PRACTICE

From Monday _____ to ⟨ Friday _____   How many times ___
          Date   next game _____   How many times ___
                              Date

1st practice was: Very easy ☐   Easy ☐   Average ☐   Hard ☐   Very hard ☐

2nd practice was: Very easy ☐   Easy ☐   Average ☐   Hard ☐   Very hard ☐

3rd practice was: Very easy ☐   Easy ☐   Average ☐   Hard ☐   Very hard ☐

1st practice: ☺ 😐 ☹   2nd practice: ☺ 😐 ☹   3rd practice: ☺ 😐 ☹

Coach focused on
_____
_____
_____

I focused on
_____
_____
_____

What I'v learnt
_____
_____

My weaknesses/strengths
_____
_____

Coach advice
_____
_____
_____

Additional notes
_____
_____

PRACTICE

From Monday _____ to < Friday _____ How many times ___
                    Date   next game _____ How many times ___
                                         Date

1st practice was: Very easy ☐ Easy ☐ Average ☐ Hard ☐ Very hard ☐

2nd practice was: Very easy ☐ Easy ☐ Average ☐ Hard ☐ Very hard ☐

3rd practice was: Very easy ☐ Easy ☐ Average ☐ Hard ☐ Very hard ☐

1st practice: ☺ 😐 ☹   2nd practice: ☺ 😐 ☹   3rd practice: ☺ 😐 ☹

Coach focused on
_____
_____
_____

I focused on
_____
_____

What I'v learnt
_____
_____

My weaknesses/strengths
_____
_____

Coach advice
_____
_____

Additional notes
_____
_____

PRACTICE

From Monday _____ to Friday _____ How many times ___
       Date   Date
                     next game _____ How many times ___
                                   Date

1st practice was: Very easy ☐ Easy ☐ Average ☐ Hard ☐ Very hard ☐
2nd practice was: Very easy ☐ Easy ☐ Average ☐ Hard ☐ Very hard ☐
3rd practice was: Very easy ☐ Easy ☐ Average ☐ Hard ☐ Very hard ☐

1st practice: ☺ ☺ ☹   2nd practice: ☺ ☺ ☹   3rd practice: ☺ ☺ ☹

Coach focused on
_____
_____
_____

I focused on
_____
_____
_____

What I'v learnt
_____
_____
_____

My weaknesses/strengths
_____
_____
_____

Coach advice
_____
_____
_____

Additional notes
_____
_____

PRACTICE

From Monday _____ to ⟨ Friday _____   How many times ___
Date   next game _____   How many times ___
                        Date

1st practice was: Very easy ☐ Easy ☐ Average ☐ Hard ☐ Very hard ☐
2nd practice was: Very easy ☐ Easy ☐ Average ☐ Hard ☐ Very hard ☐
3rd practice was: Very easy ☐ Easy ☐ Average ☐ Hard ☐ Very hard ☐

1st practice: ☺ 😐 ☹   2nd practice: ☺ 😐 ☹   3rd practice: ☺ 😐 ☹

Coach focused on
_____
_____
_____

I focused on
_____
_____
_____

What I'v learnt
_____
_____
_____

My weaknesses/strengths
_____
_____
_____

Coach advice
_____
_____
_____

Additional notes
_____
_____

PRACTICE

From Monday _____ to <Friday _____   How many times ___
Date

next game _____   How many times ___
Date

1st practice was: Very easy ☐   Easy ☐   Average ☐   Hard ☐   Very hard ☐

2nd practice was: Very easy ☐   Easy ☐   Average ☐   Hard ☐   Very hard ☐

3rd practice was: Very easy ☐   Easy ☐   Average ☐   Hard ☐   Very hard ☐

1st practice: 🙂 😐 🙁   2nd practice: 🙂 😐 🙁   3rd practice: 🙂 😐 🙁

Coach focused on
_____
_____
_____

I focused on
_____
_____
_____

What I'v learnt
_____
_____
_____

My weaknesses/strengths
_____
_____
_____

Coach advice
_____
_____
_____

Additional notes
_____
_____
_____

PRACTICE

From Monday _____ to Friday _____ How many times ___
Date   next game _____ How many times ___
                  Date   Date

1st practice was: Very easy ☐ Easy ☐ Average ☐ Hard ☐ Very hard ☐
2nd practice was: Very easy ☐ Easy ☐ Average ☐ Hard ☐ Very hard ☐
3rd practice was: Very easy ☐ Easy ☐ Average ☐ Hard ☐ Very hard ☐

1st practice: ☺ 😐 ☹ 2nd practice: ☺ 😐 ☹ 3rd practice: ☺ 😐 ☹

Coach focused on
_____
_____
_____

I focused on
_____
_____
_____

What I'v learnt
_____
_____
_____

My weaknesses/strengths
_____
_____

Coach advice
_____
_____
_____

Additional notes
_____
_____

PRACTICE

From Monday _____ to $\lbrace$ Friday _____ How many times ___
                           next game _____ How many times ___
                   Date   Date

1st practice was: Very easy ☐ Easy ☐ Average ☐ Hard ☐ Very hard ☐
2nd practice was: Very easy ☐ Easy ☐ Average ☐ Hard ☐ Very hard ☐
3rd practice was: Very easy ☐ Easy ☐ Average ☐ Hard ☐ Very hard ☐

1st practice: ☺ 😐 ☹   2nd practice: ☺ 😐 ☹   3rd practice: ☺ 😐 ☹

Coach focused on
_____
_____
_____

I focused on
_____
_____
_____

What I'v learnt
_____
_____
_____

My weaknesses/strengths
_____
_____
_____

Coach advice
_____
_____
_____

Additional notes
_____
_____

PRACTICE

From Monday _____ to ⟨ Friday _____   How many times ___
          Date   next game _____   How many times ___
                                    Date

1st practice was: Very easy ☐ Easy ☐ Average ☐ Hard ☐ Very hard ☐

2nd practice was: Very easy ☐ Easy ☐ Average ☐ Hard ☐ Very hard ☐

3rd practice was: Very easy ☐ Easy ☐ Average ☐ Hard ☐ Very hard ☐

1st practice: ☺ 😐 ☹   2nd practice: ☺ 😐 ☹   3rd practice: ☺ 😐 ☹

Coach focused on _____
_____
_____
_____

I focused on _____
_____
_____

What I'v learnt _____
_____
_____

My weaknesses/strengths _____
_____
_____

Coach advice _____
_____
_____

Additional notes _____
_____
_____

PRACTICE

From Monday _____ to Friday _____ How many times ___
From Monday (Date) to next game _____ How many times ___
                                    (Date)

1st practice was: Very easy ☐ Easy ☐ Average ☐ Hard ☐ Very hard ☐
2nd practice was: Very easy ☐ Easy ☐ Average ☐ Hard ☐ Very hard ☐
3rd practice was: Very easy ☐ Easy ☐ Average ☐ Hard ☐ Very hard ☐

1st practice: ☺ 😐 ☹   2nd practice: ☺ 😐 ☹   3rd practice: ☺ 😐 ☹

Coach focused on
_____
_____
_____

I focused on
_____
_____
_____

What I'v learnt
_____
_____
_____

My weaknesses/strengths
_____
_____
_____

Coach advice
_____
_____
_____

Additional notes
_____
_____

PRACTICE

From Monday _____ to ┌ Friday _____   How many times ___
Date   └ next game _____   How many times ___
Date

1st practice was: Very easy ☐ Easy ☐ Average ☐ Hard ☐ Very hard ☐

2nd practice was: Very easy ☐ Easy ☐ Average ☐ Hard ☐ Very hard ☐

3rd practice was: Very easy ☐ Easy ☐ Average ☐ Hard ☐ Very hard ☐

1st practice: ☺ 😐 ☹   2nd practice: ☺ 😐 ☹   3rd practice: ☺ 😐 ☹

Coach focused on
_____
_____
_____

I focused on
_____
_____
_____

What I'v learnt
_____
_____
_____

My weaknesses/strengths
_____
_____

Coach advice
_____
_____
_____

Additional notes
_____
_____
_____

PRACTICE

From Monday _____ to Friday _____ How many times ___
               Date   Date
                         next game _____ How many times ___
                                          Date

1st practice was: Very easy ☐ Easy ☐ Average ☐ Hard ☐ Very hard ☐

2nd practice was: Very easy ☐ Easy ☐ Average ☐ Hard ☐ Very hard ☐

3rd practice was: Very easy ☐ Easy ☐ Average ☐ Hard ☐ Very hard ☐

1st practice: ☺ 😐 ☹   2nd practice: ☺ 😐 ☹   3rd practice: ☺ 😐 ☹

Coach focused on
_____
_____
_____

I focused on
_____
_____
_____

What I'v learnt
_____
_____
_____

My weaknesses/strengths
_____
_____
_____

Coach advice
_____
_____
_____

Additional notes
_____
_____
_____

PRACTICE

From Monday _____ to < Friday _____ How many times ___
                Date   Date
                        next game _____ How many times ___
                                        Date

1st practice was: Very easy ☐ Easy ☐ Average ☐ Hard ☐ Very hard ☐

2nd practice was: Very easy ☐ Easy ☐ Average ☐ Hard ☐ Very hard ☐

3rd practice was: Very easy ☐ Easy ☐ Average ☐ Hard ☐ Very hard ☐

1st practice: 🙂 😐 ☹️   2nd practice: 🙂 😐 ☹️   3rd practice: 🙂 😐 ☹️

Coach focused on
_____
_____
_____
_____

I focused on
_____
_____
_____

What I'v learnt
_____
_____
_____

My weaknesses/strengths
_____
_____
_____

Coach advice
_____
_____
_____

Additional notes
_____
_____

PRACTICE

From Monday _____ to < Friday _____ How many times ___
                          Date
                          next game _____ How many times ___
                          Date

1st practice was: Very easy ☐ Easy ☐ Average ☐ Hard ☐ Very hard ☐
2nd practice was: Very easy ☐ Easy ☐ Average ☐ Hard ☐ Very hard ☐
3rd practice was: Very easy ☐ Easy ☐ Average ☐ Hard ☐ Very hard ☐

1st practice: 🙂 😐 🙁 2nd practice: 🙂 😐 🙁 3rd practice: 🙂 😐 🙁

Coach focused on _____
_____
_____

I focused on _____
_____
_____

What I'v learnt _____
_____
_____

My weaknesses/strengths _____
_____
_____

Coach advice _____
_____
_____

Additional notes _____
_____
_____

PRACTICE

From Monday _____ to Friday _____ How many times ___
                    Date   Date
              next game _____ How many times ___
                            Date

1st practice was: Very easy ☐ Easy ☐ Average ☐ Hard ☐ Very hard ☐

2nd practice was: Very easy ☐ Easy ☐ Average ☐ Hard ☐ Very hard ☐

3rd practice was: Very easy ☐ Easy ☐ Average ☐ Hard ☐ Very hard ☐

1st practice: ☺ 😐 ☹   2nd practice: ☺ 😐 ☹   3rd practice: ☺ 😐 ☹

Coach focused on
_____
_____
_____

I focused on
_____
_____
_____

What I'v learnt
_____
_____
_____

My weaknesses/strengths
_____
_____
_____

Coach advice
_____
_____
_____

Additional notes
_____
_____
_____

PRACTICE

From Monday _____ to Friday _____ How many times ___
Date
next game _____ How many times ___
Date

1st practice was: Very easy ☐ Easy ☐ Average ☐ Hard ☐ Very hard ☐

2nd practice was: Very easy ☐ Easy ☐ Average ☐ Hard ☐ Very hard ☐

3rd practice was: Very easy ☐ Easy ☐ Average ☐ Hard ☐ Very hard ☐

1st practice: ☺ 😐 ☹ 2nd practice: ☺ 😐 ☹ 3rd practice: ☺ 😐 ☹

Coach focused on _____
_____
_____
_____

I focused on _____
_____
_____

What I'v learnt _____
_____
_____

My weaknesses/strengths _____
_____
_____

Coach advice _____
_____
_____

Additional notes _____
_____
_____

PRACTICE

From Monday _____ to Friday _____ How many times ___
Date   Date

next game _____ How many times ___
Date

1st practice was: Very easy ☐ Easy ☐ Average ☐ Hard ☐ Very hard ☐

2nd practice was: Very easy ☐ Easy ☐ Average ☐ Hard ☐ Very hard ☐

3rd practice was: Very easy ☐ Easy ☐ Average ☐ Hard ☐ Very hard ☐

1st practice: ☺ 😐 ☹   2nd practice: ☺ 😐 ☹   3rd practice: ☺ 😐 ☹

Coach focused on
_____
_____
_____

I focused on
_____
_____
_____

What I'v learnt
_____
_____
_____

My weaknesses/strengths
_____
_____
_____

Coach advice
_____
_____
_____

Additional notes
_____
_____
_____

GAME DAY

Date _____   Tournament ☐

Against _____ Time _____

Score - W D L _____   1st/2nd period score _____ /_____ Home ☐ Away ☐

Position _____   Mood before match: ☺ 😐 ☹

Match was: Very easy ☐   Easy ☐   Average ☐   Hard ☐   Very hard ☐

Evaluation of my:

- warm up _____

_____

- effort and work rate level _____

_____

_____

- speed _____

- spacing _____

_____

- decision making with the ball under pressure _____

_____

_____

Good parts of my play were _____

_____

_____

_____

What I could do better _____

_____

_____

I rate my performance today as_____

What I want to improve upon in practice _____

_____

GAME DAY

Date _____   Tournament ☐

Against _____ Time _____
Score - W D L _____ 1st/2nd period score _____ /_____ Home☐ Away☐
Position _____ Mood before match: 😊 😐 ☹
Match was: Very easy☐ Easy☐ Average☐ Hard☐ Very hard☐
Evaluation of my:

- warm up _____
_____

- effort and work rate level _____
_____
_____

- speed _____
- spacing _____
_____

- decision making with the ball under pressure_____
_____
_____

Good parts of my play were _____
_____
_____
_____

What I could do better _____
_____
_____

I rate my performance today as_____
What I want to improve upon in practice _____
_____
_____

GAME DAY

Date _____ **GAME DAY** Tournament ☐

Against _____ Time _____

Score - W D L _____ 1st/2nd period score _____ /_____ Home ☐ Away ☐

Position _____ Mood before match: ☺ 😐 ☹

Match was: Very easy ☐   Easy ☐   Average ☐   Hard ☐   Very hard ☐

Evaluation of my:

- warm up _____

_____

- effort and work rate level _____

_____

_____

- speed _____

- spacing _____

_____

- decision making with the ball under pressure_____

_____

_____

Good parts of my play were _____

_____

_____

_____

What I could do better _____

_____

_____

I rate my performance today as_____

What I want to improve upon in practice _____

_____

_____

GAME DAY

Date _____   Tournament ☐

Against _____ Time _____

Score - W D L _____ 1st/2nd period score _____ /_____ Home ☐ Away ☐

Position _____   Mood before match: 🙂 😐 ☹️

Match was: Very easy ☐   Easy ☐   Average ☐   Hard ☐   Very hard ☐

Evaluation of my:

- warm up _____

_____

- effort and work rate level _____

_____

_____

- speed _____

- spacing _____

_____

- decision making with the ball under pressure_____

_____

_____

Good parts of my play were _____

_____

_____

_____

What I could do better _____

_____

_____

I rate my performance today as_____

What I want to improve upon in practice _____

_____

_____

GAME DAY

Date _____   Tournament ☐

Against _____ Time _____

Score - W D L_____   1st/2nd period score _____ /_____ Home ☐ Away ☐

Position _____ Mood before match: ☺ 😐 ☹

Match was: Very easy ☐   Easy ☐   Average ☐   Hard ☐   Very hard ☐

Evaluation of my:

- warm up _____

_____

- effort and work rate level _____

_____

_____

- speed _____

- spacing _____

_____

- decision making with the ball under pressure_____

_____

_____

Good parts of my play were _____

_____

_____

What I could do better _____

_____

_____

I rate my performance today as_____

What I want to improve upon in practice _____

_____

_____

GAME DAY

Date _____ Tournament ☐

Against _____ Time _____

Score - W D L _____ 1st/2nd period score _____ /_____ Home☐ Away☐

Position _____ Mood before match: ☺ ☺ ☹

Match was: Very easy☐   Easy☐   Average☐   Hard☐   Very hard☐

Evaluation of my:

   - warm up _____

_____

   - effort and work rate level _____

_____

_____

   - speed _____

   - spacing _____

_____

   - decision making with the ball under pressure_____

_____

_____

Good parts of my play were _____

_____

_____

What I could do better _____

_____

_____

I rate my performance today as_____

What I want to improve upon in practice _____

_____

_____

GAME DAY

Date _____   Tournament ☐

Against _____   Time _____

Score - W D L _____   1st/2nd period score _____ /_____ Home☐ Away☐

Position _____   Mood before match: ☺ 😐 ☹

Match was: Very easy☐   Easy☐   Average☐   Hard☐   Very hard☐

Evaluation of my:

- warm up _____

_____

- effort and work rate level _____

_____

_____

- speed _____

- spacing _____

_____

- decision making with the ball under pressure_____

_____

_____

Good parts of my play were _____

_____

_____

What I could do better _____

_____

_____

I rate my performance today as_____

What I want to improve upon in practice _____

_____

_____

GAME DAY

Date _____

Tournament ☐

Against _____ Time _____

Score - W D L_____   1st/2nd period score ____ /____ Home☐ Away☐

Position _____   Mood before match: ☺ ☺ ☹

Match was: Very easy☐   Easy☐   Average☐   Hard☐   Very hard☐

Evaluation of my:

- warm up _____

_____

- effort and work rate level _____

_____

_____

- speed _____

- spacing _____

_____

- decision making with the ball under pressure_____

_____

_____

Good parts of my play were _____

_____

_____

What I could do better _____

_____

_____

I rate my performance today as_____

What I want to improve upon in practice _____

_____

_____

GAME DAY

Date _____   Tournament ☐

Against _____ Time _____

Score - W D L _____ 1st/2nd period score _____ /_____ Home ☐ Away ☐

Position _____ Mood before match: ☺ 😐 ☹

Match was: Very easy ☐   Easy ☐   Average ☐   Hard ☐   Very hard ☐

Evaluation of my:

- warm up _____

_____

- effort and work rate level _____

_____

_____

- speed _____

- spacing _____

_____

- decision making with the ball under pressure _____

_____

_____

Good parts of my play were _____

_____

_____

_____

What I could do better _____

_____

_____

I rate my performance today as_____

What I want to improve upon in practice _____

_____

_____

GAME DAY

Date _____   Tournament ☐

Against _____ Time _____

Score - W D L _____   1st/2nd period score _____ /_____ Home☐ Away☐

Position _____   Mood before match: ☺ 😐 ☹

Match was: Very easy☐   Easy☐   Average☐   Hard☐   Very hard☐

Evaluation of my:

   - warm up _____

_____

   - effort and work rate level _____

_____

_____

   - speed _____

   - spacing _____

_____

   - decision making with the ball under pressure_____

_____

_____

Good parts of my play were _____

_____

_____

_____

What I could do better _____

_____

_____

I rate my performance today as_____

What I want to improve upon in practice _____

_____

_____

PRACTICE

From Monday _____ to < Friday _____ How many times ___
                Date   next game _____ How many times ___
                                    Date

1st practice was: Very easy ☐ Easy ☐ Average ☐ Hard ☐ Very hard ☐
2nd practice was: Very easy ☐ Easy ☐ Average ☐ Hard ☐ Very hard ☐
3rd practice was: Very easy ☐ Easy ☐ Average ☐ Hard ☐ Very hard ☐

1st practice: ☺ 😐 ☹   2nd practice: ☺ 😐 ☹   3rd practice: ☺ 😐 ☹

Coach focused on
_____
_____
_____

I focused on
_____
_____
_____

What I'v learnt
_____
_____
_____

My weaknesses/strengths
_____
_____

Coach advice
_____
_____
_____

Additional notes
_____
_____

GAME DAY

Date _____   Tournament ☐

Against _____ Time _____

Score - W D L _____   1st/2nd period score _____ /_____ Home☐ Away☐

Position _____   Mood before match: ☺ 😐 ☹

Match was: Very easy☐   Easy☐   Average☐   Hard☐   Very hard☐

Evaluation of my:

- warm up _____

_____

- effort and work rate level _____

_____

_____

- speed _____

- spacing _____

_____

- decision making with the ball under pressure_____

_____

_____

Good parts of my play were _____

_____

_____

_____

What I could do better _____

_____

_____

I rate my performance today as_____

What I want to improve upon in practice _____

_____

_____

GAME DAY

Date _____ Tournament ☐

Against _____ Time _____

Score - W D L _____ 1st/2nd period score _____ /_____ Home ☐ Away ☐

Position _____ Mood before match: ☺ 😐 ☹

Match was: Very easy ☐ Easy ☐ Average ☐ Hard ☐ Very hard ☐

Evaluation of my:

- warm up _____

_____

- effort and work rate level _____

_____

_____

- speed _____
- spacing _____

_____

- decision making with the ball under pressure_____

_____

_____

Good parts of my play were _____

_____

_____

What I could do better _____

_____

_____

I rate my performance today as_____

What I want to improve upon in practice _____

_____

GAME DAY

Date _____

Tournament ☐

Against _____ Time _____

Score - W D L _____ 1st/2nd period score _____ /_____ Home ☐ Away ☐

Position _____ Mood before match: ☺ 😐 ☹

Match was: Very easy ☐ Easy ☐ Average ☐ Hard ☐ Very hard ☐

Evaluation of my:

- warm up _____

_____

- effort and work rate level _____

_____

_____

- speed _____

- spacing _____

_____

- decision making with the ball under pressure_____

_____

_____

Good parts of my play were _____

_____

_____

_____

What I could do better _____

_____

_____

I rate my performance today as_____

What I want to improve upon in practice _____

_____

_____

GAME DAY

Date _____   Tournament ☐

Against _____ Time _____

Score - W D L _____   1st/2nd period score _____ /_____ Home☐ Away☐

Position _____   Mood before match: ☺ ☻ ☹

Match was: Very easy☐   Easy☐   Average☐   Hard☐   Very hard☐

Evaluation of my:

- warm up _____

_____

- effort and work rate level _____

_____

_____

- speed _____

- spacing _____

_____

- decision making with the ball under pressure_____

_____

_____

Good parts of my play were _____

_____

_____

_____

What I could do better _____

_____

_____

I rate my performance today as_____

What I want to improve upon in practice _____

_____

_____

GAME DAY

Date _____ **GAME DAY** Tournament ☐

Against _____ Time _____

Score - W D L _____ 1st/2nd period score _____ /_____ Home ☐ Away ☐

Position _____ Mood before match: ☺ 😐 ☹

Match was: Very easy ☐   Easy ☐   Average ☐   Hard ☐   Very hard ☐

Evaluation of my:

- warm up _____

_____

- effort and work rate level _____

_____

_____

- speed _____

- spacing _____

_____

- decision making with the ball under pressure _____

_____

_____

Good parts of my play were _____

_____

_____

_____

What I could do better _____

_____

_____

I rate my performance today as _____

What I want to improve upon in practice _____

_____

_____

GAME DAY

Date _____   Tournament ☐

Against _____ Time _____

Score - W D L _____ 1st/2nd period score _____ / ____ Home ☐ Away ☐

Position _____ Mood before match: ☺ 😐 ☹

Match was: Very easy ☐ Easy ☐ Average ☐ Hard ☐ Very hard ☐

Evaluation of my:

- warm up _____

_____

- effort and work rate level _____

_____

_____

- speed _____

- spacing _____

_____

- decision making with the ball under pressure_____

_____

_____

Good parts of my play were _____

_____

_____

What I could do better _____

_____

_____

I rate my performance today as_____

What I want to improve upon in practice _____

_____

_____

GAME DAY

Date _____

Tournament ☐

Against _____ Time _____

Score - W D L _____   1st/2nd period score _____ /_____ Home☐ Away☐

Position _____   Mood before match: ☺ 😐 ☹

Match was: Very easy☐   Easy☐   Average☐   Hard☐   Very hard☐

Evaluation of my:

- warm up _____

_____

- effort and work rate level _____

_____

_____

- speed _____
- spacing _____

_____

- decision making with the ball under pressure_____

_____

_____

Good parts of my play were _____

_____

_____

What I could do better _____

_____

_____

I rate my performance today as_____

What I want to improve upon in practice _____

_____

GAME DAY

Date _____ Tournament ☐

Against _____ Time _____

Score - W D L _____ 1st/2nd period score _____ / _____ Home ☐ Away ☐

Position _____ Mood before match: ☺ 😐 ☹

Match was: Very easy ☐   Easy ☐   Average ☐   Hard ☐   Very hard ☐

Evaluation of my:

- warm up _____

_____

- effort and work rate level _____

_____

_____

- speed _____

- spacing _____

_____

- decision making with the ball under pressure _____

_____

_____

Good parts of my play were _____

_____

_____

_____

What I could do better _____

_____

_____

I rate my performance today as_____

What I want to improve upon in practice _____

_____

_____

GAME DAY

Date _____   Tournament ☐

Against _____ Time _____

Score - W D L _____   1st/2nd period score _____ /_____ Home☐ Away☐

Position _____   Mood before match: ☺ 😐 ☹

Match was: Very easy☐   Easy☐   Average☐   Hard☐   Very hard☐

Evaluation of my:

- warm up _____

_____

- effort and work rate level _____

_____

_____

- speed _____
- spacing _____

_____

- decision making with the ball under pressure_____

_____

_____

Good parts of my play were _____

_____

_____

_____

What I could do better _____

_____

_____

I rate my performance today as_____

What I want to improve upon in practice _____

_____

_____

GAME DAY

Date _____

Tournament ☐

Against _____ Time _____

Score - W D L _____ 1st/2nd period score _____ /_____ Home ☐ Away ☐

Position _____ Mood before match: ☺ 😐 ☹

Match was: Very easy ☐ Easy ☐ Average ☐ Hard ☐ Very hard ☐

Evaluation of my:

- warm up _____

_____

- effort and work rate level _____

_____

_____

- speed _____

- spacing _____

_____

- decision making with the ball under pressure _____

_____

_____

Good parts of my play were _____

_____

_____

_____

What I could do better _____

_____

_____

I rate my performance today as_____

What I want to improve upon in practice _____

_____

_____

PRACTICE

From Monday _____ to < Friday _____   How many times ___
                         Date
                         next game _____   How many times ___
                            Date

1st practice was: Very easy ☐ Easy ☐ Average ☐ Hard ☐ Very hard ☐

2nd practice was: Very easy ☐ Easy ☐ Average ☐ Hard ☐ Very hard ☐

3rd practice was: Very easy ☐ Easy ☐ Average ☐ Hard ☐ Very hard ☐

1st practice: ☺ 😐 ☹   2nd practice: ☺ 😐 ☹   3rd practice: ☺ 😐 ☹

Coach focused on _____
_____
_____

I focused on _____
_____
_____

What I'v learnt _____
_____
_____

My weaknesses/strengths _____
_____
_____

Coach advice _____
_____
_____

Additional notes _____
_____
_____

GAME DAY

Date _____   Tournament ☐

Against _____ Time _____

Score - W D L _____ 1st/2nd period score _____ / _____ Home☐ Away☐

Position _____ Mood before match: ☺ 😐 ☹

Match was: Very easy☐   Easy☐   Average☐   Hard☐   Very hard☐

Evaluation of my:

- warm up _____

_____

- effort and work rate level _____

_____

_____

- speed _____

- spacing _____

_____

- decision making with the ball under pressure_____

_____

_____

Good parts of my play were _____

_____

_____

What I could do better _____

_____

_____

I rate my performance today as_____

What I want to improve upon in practice _____

_____

_____

GAME DAY

Date _____ Tournament ☐

Against _____ Time _____

Score - W D L _____ 1st/2nd period score _____ /____ Home ☐ Away ☐

Position _____ Mood before match: ☺ ☺ ☹

Match was: Very easy ☐   Easy ☐   Average ☐   Hard ☐   Very hard ☐

Evaluation of my:

- warm up _____

_____

- effort and work rate level _____

_____

_____

- speed _____

- spacing _____

_____

- decision making with the ball under pressure_____

_____

_____

Good parts of my play were _____

_____

_____

_____

What I could do better _____

_____

_____

I rate my performance today as_____

What I want to improve upon in practice _____

_____

GAME DAY

Date _____   Tournament ☐

Against _____ Time _____

Score - W D L _____   1st/2nd period score _____ / _____ Home ☐ Away ☐

Position _____   Mood before match: ☺ 😐 ☹

Match was: Very easy ☐   Easy ☐   Average ☐   Hard ☐   Very hard ☐

Evaluation of my:

- warm up _____

_____

- effort and work rate level _____

_____

_____

- speed _____
- spacing _____

_____

- decision making with the ball under pressure _____

_____

_____

Good parts of my play were _____

_____

_____

_____

What I could do better _____

_____

_____

I rate my performance today as_____

What I want to improve upon in practice _____

_____

_____

GAME DAY

Date _____   Tournament ☐

Against _____ Time _____

Score - W D L _____ 1st/2nd period score _____ /_____ Home☐ Away☐

Position _____   Mood before match: ☺ 😐 ☹

Match was: Very easy☐ Easy☐ Average☐ Hard☐ Very hard☐

Evaluation of my:

- warm up _____

_____

- effort and work rate level _____

_____

_____

- speed _____

- spacing _____

_____

- decision making with the ball under pressure_____

_____

Good parts of my play were _____

_____

_____

What I could do better _____

_____

I rate my performance today as_____

What I want to improve upon in practice _____

_____

GAME DAY

Date _____   Tournament ☐

Against _____ Time _____

Score - W D L _____   1st/2nd period score _____ /_____ Home☐ Away☐

Position _____   Mood before match: ☺ 😐 ☹

Match was: Very easy☐   Easy☐   Average☐   Hard☐   Very hard☐

Evaluation of my:

    - warm up _____

_____

    - effort and work rate level _____

_____

_____

     - speed _____

     - spacing _____

_____

    - decision making with the ball under pressure_____

_____

_____

Good parts of my play were _____

_____

_____

What I could do better _____

_____

_____

I rate my performance today as_____

What I want to improve upon in practice _____

_____

_____

GAME DAY

Date _____   Tournament ☐

Against _____ Time _____

Score - W D L _____ 1st/2nd period score _____ /_____ Home ☐ Away ☐

Position _____   Mood before match: ☺ ☺ ☹

Match was: Very easy ☐   Easy ☐   Average ☐   Hard ☐   Very hard ☐

Evaluation of my:

- warm up _____

_____

- effort and work rate level _____

_____

_____

- speed _____

- spacing _____

_____

- decision making with the ball under pressure _____

_____

_____

Good parts of my play were _____

_____

_____

_____

What I could do better _____

_____

_____

I rate my performance today as _____

What I want to improve upon in practice _____

_____

_____

GAME DAY

Date _____   Tournament ☐

Against _____ Time _____

Score - W D L _____   1st/2nd period score _____ /_____ Home ☐ Away ☐

Position _____   Mood before match: ☺ 😐 ☹

Match was: Very easy ☐   Easy ☐   Average ☐   Hard ☐   Very hard ☐

Evaluation of my:

- warm up _____

_____

- effort and work rate level _____

_____

_____

- speed _____

- spacing _____

_____

- decision making with the ball under pressure _____

_____

_____

Good parts of my play were _____

_____

_____

_____

What I could do better _____

_____

_____

I rate my performance today as_____

What I want to improve upon in practice _____

_____

_____

GAME DAY

Date _____

Tournament ☐

Against _____ Time _____

Score - W D L _____ 1st/2nd period score _____ /_____ Home☐ Away☐

Position _____ Mood before match: ☺ 😐 ☹

Match was: Very easy☐ Easy☐ Average☐ Hard☐ Very hard☐

Evaluation of my:

- warm up _____

_____

- effort and work rate level _____

_____

_____

- speed _____

- spacing _____

_____

- decision making with the ball under pressure_____

_____

_____

Good parts of my play were _____

_____

_____

_____

What I could do better _____

_____

_____

I rate my performance today as_____

What I want to improve upon in practice _____

_____

GAME DAY

Date _____   Tournament ☐

Against _____ Time _____

Score - W D L _____ 1st/2nd period score _____ / _____ Home ☐ Away ☐

Position _____ Mood before match: ☺ 😐 ☹

Match was: Very easy ☐ Easy ☐ Average ☐ Hard ☐ Very hard ☐

Evaluation of my:

- warm up _____

_____

- effort and work rate level _____

_____

_____

- speed _____

- spacing _____

_____

- decision making with the ball under pressure_____

_____

Good parts of my play were _____

_____

_____

_____

What I could do better _____

_____

_____

I rate my performance today as_____

What I want to improve upon in practice _____

_____

_____

GAME DAY

Date _____   Tournament ☐

Against _____ Time _____

Score - W D L _____   1st/2nd period score _____ /_____ Home☐ Away☐

Position _____   Mood before match: ☺ 😐 ☹

Match was: Very easy☐   Easy☐   Average☐   Hard☐   Very hard☐

Evaluation of my:

- warm up _____

_____

- effort and work rate level _____

_____

_____

- speed _____

- spacing _____

_____

- decision making with the ball under pressure_____

_____

_____

Good parts of my play were _____

_____

_____

_____

What I could do better _____

_____

_____

I rate my performance today as_____

What I want to improve upon in practice _____

_____

_____

PRACTICE

From Monday _____ to ⟨ Friday _____   How many times ___
                  Date   Date
                        next game _____   How many times ___
                                         Date

1st practice was: Very easy ☐ Easy ☐ Average ☐ Hard ☐ Very hard ☐

2nd practice was: Very easy ☐ Easy ☐ Average ☐ Hard ☐ Very hard ☐

3rd practice was: Very easy ☐ Easy ☐ Average ☐ Hard ☐ Very hard ☐

1st practice: ☺ 😐 ☹   2nd practice: ☺ 😐 ☹   3rd practice: ☺ 😐 ☹

Coach focused on
_____
_____
_____
_____

I focused on
_____
_____
_____

What I'v learnt
_____
_____
_____

My weaknesses/strengths
_____
_____
_____

Coach advice
_____
_____
_____

Additional notes
_____
_____

GAME DAY

Date _____ Tournament ☐

Against _____ Time _____

Score - W D L _____ 1st/2nd period score _____ /_____ Home☐ Away☐

Position _____ Mood before match: ☺ 😐 ☹

Match was: Very easy☐ Easy☐ Average☐ Hard☐ Very hard☐

Evaluation of my:

- warm up _____

_____

- effort and work rate level _____

_____

_____

- speed _____

- spacing _____

_____

- decision making with the ball under pressure_____

_____

_____

Good parts of my play were _____

_____

_____

_____

What I could do better _____

_____

_____

I rate my performance today as_____

What I want to improve upon in practice _____

_____

_____

GAME DAY

Date _____   Tournament ☐

Against _____ Time _____

Score - W D L _____   1st/2nd period score _____ / _____ Home ☐ Away ☐

Position _____   Mood before match: ☺ 😐 ☹

Match was: Very easy ☐   Easy ☐   Average ☐   Hard ☐   Very hard ☐

Evaluation of my:

   - warm up _____

_____

   - effort and work rate level _____

_____

_____

   - speed _____

   - spacing _____

_____

   - decision making with the ball under pressure_____

_____

Good parts of my play were _____

_____

_____

What I could do better _____

_____

_____

I rate my performance today as_____

What I want to improve upon in practice _____

_____

_____

GAME DAY

Date _____   Tournament ☐

Against _____   Time _____

Score - W D L _____   1st/2nd period score _____ /_____ Home☐ Away☐

Position _____   Mood before match: 🙂 😐 🙁

Match was: Very easy☐   Easy☐   Average☐   Hard☐   Very hard☐

Evaluation of my:

- warm up _____

_____

- effort and work rate level _____

_____

_____

- speed _____

- spacing _____

_____

- decision making with the ball under pressure_____

_____

_____

Good parts of my play were _____

_____

_____

What I could do better _____

_____

_____

I rate my performance today as_____

What I want to improve upon in practice _____

_____

_____

GAME DAY

Date _____   **GAME DAY**   Tournament ☐

Against _____ Time _____

Score - W D L _____ 1st/2nd period score _____ /_____ Home☐ Away☐

Position _____ Mood before match: ☺ 😐 ☹

Match was: Very easy☐   Easy☐   Average☐   Hard☐   Very hard☐

Evaluation of my:

- warm up _____

_____

- effort and work rate level _____

_____

_____

- speed _____
- spacing _____

_____

- decision making with the ball under pressure_____

_____

_____

Good parts of my play were _____

_____

_____

What I could do better _____

_____

_____

I rate my performance today as_____

What I want to improve upon in practice _____

_____

_____

GAME DAY

Date _____ Tournament ☐

Against _____ Time _____

Score - W D L _____ 1st/2nd period score _____ /_____ Home ☐ Away ☐

Position _____ Mood before match: 🙂 😐 🙁

Match was: Very easy ☐   Easy ☐   Average ☐   Hard ☐   Very hard ☐

Evaluation of my:

- warm up _____

_____

- effort and work rate level _____

_____

_____

- speed _____

- spacing _____

_____

- decision making with the ball under pressure _____

_____

_____

Good parts of my play were _____

_____

_____

_____

What I could do better _____

_____

_____

I rate my performance today as _____

What I want to improve upon in practice _____

_____

_____

GAME DAY

Date _____   Tournament ☐

Against _____   Time _____

Score - W D L _____   1st/2nd period score _____ /_____   Home☐ Away☐

Position _____   Mood before match: ☺ 😐 ☹

Match was: Very easy☐   Easy☐   Average☐   Hard☐   Very hard☐

Evaluation of my:

- warm up _____

_____

- effort and work rate level _____

_____

_____

- speed _____
- spacing _____

_____

- decision making with the ball under pressure_____

_____

_____

Good parts of my play were _____

_____

_____

_____

What I could do better _____

_____

_____

I rate my performance today as_____

What I want to improve upon in practice _____

_____

_____

GAME DAY

Date _____

Tournament ☐

Against _____ Time _____

Score - W D L _____ 1st/2nd period score _____ /_____ Home ☐ Away ☐

Position _____ Mood before match: 🙂 😐 🙁

Match was: Very easy ☐   Easy ☐   Average ☐   Hard ☐   Very hard ☐

Evaluation of my:

- warm up _____

_____

- effort and work rate level _____

_____

_____

- speed _____

- spacing _____

_____

- decision making with the ball under pressure _____

_____

_____

Good parts of my play were _____

_____

_____

_____

What I could do better _____

_____

_____

I rate my performance today as_____

What I want to improve upon in practice _____

_____

_____

GAME DAY

Date _____   Tournament ☐

Against _____ Time _____

Score - W D L _____ 1st/2nd period score _____ /_____ Home ☐ Away ☐

Position _____   Mood before match: 😊 😐 ☹

Match was: Very easy ☐   Easy ☐   Average ☐   Hard ☐   Very hard ☐

Evaluation of my:

- warm up _____

_____

- effort and work rate level _____

_____

_____

- speed _____

- spacing _____

_____

- decision making with the ball under pressure_____

_____

_____

Good parts of my play were _____

_____

_____

What I could do better _____

_____

_____

I rate my performance today as_____

What I want to improve upon in practice _____

_____

GAME DAY

Date _____   Tournament ☐

Against _____ Time _____

Score - W D L _____ 1st/2nd period score _____ /_____ Home☐ Away☐

Position _____ Mood before match: 😊 😐 😞

Match was: Very easy☐ Easy☐ Average☐ Hard☐ Very hard☐

Evaluation of my:

- warm up _____

_____

- effort and work rate level _____

_____

_____

- speed _____

- spacing _____

_____

- decision making with the ball under pressure_____

_____

_____

Good parts of my play were _____

_____

_____

_____

What I could do better _____

_____

_____

I rate my performance today as_____

What I want to improve upon in practice _____

_____

_____

GAME DAY

Date _____   Tournament ☐

Against _____ Time _____

Score - W D L _____   1st/2nd period score _____ / _____   Home ☐ Away ☐

Position _____   Mood before match: ☺ 😐 ☹

Match was: Very easy ☐   Easy ☐   Average ☐   Hard ☐   Very hard ☐

Evaluation of my:

    - warm up _____

_____

    - effort and work rate level _____

_____

_____

    - speed _____

    - spacing _____

_____

    - decision making with the ball under pressure _____

_____

_____

Good parts of my play were _____

_____

_____

_____

What I could do better _____

_____

_____

I rate my performance today as _____

What I want to improve upon in practice _____

_____

_____

PRACTICE

From Monday _____ to Friday _____ How many times ___
                      Date   Date
                 next game _____ How many times ___
                              Date

1st practice was: Very easy ☐ Easy ☐ Average ☐ Hard ☐ Very hard ☐

2nd practice was: Very easy ☐ Easy ☐ Average ☐ Hard ☐ Very hard ☐

3rd practice was: Very easy ☐ Easy ☐ Average ☐ Hard ☐ Very hard ☐

1st practice: 🙂 😐 🙁   2nd practice: 🙂 😐 🙁   3rd practice: 🙂 😐 🙁

Coach focused on
_____
_____
_____

I focused on
_____
_____

What I'v learnt
_____
_____

My weaknesses/strengths
_____
_____

Coach advice
_____
_____

Additional notes
_____
_____

GAME DAY

Date _____   Tournament ☐

Against _____ Time _____

Score - W D L _____   1st/2nd period score _____ /_____ Home ☐ Away ☐

Position _____   Mood before match: ☺ 😐 ☹

Match was: Very easy ☐   Easy ☐   Average ☐   Hard ☐   Very hard ☐

Evaluation of my:

    - warm up _____

_____

     - effort and work rate level _____

_____

_____

     - speed _____

     - spacing _____

_____

     - decision making with the ball under pressure_____

_____

_____

Good parts of my play were _____

_____

_____

What I could do better _____

_____

_____

I rate my performance today as_____

What I want to improve upon in practice _____

_____

_____

GAME DAY

Date _____   Tournament ☐

Against _____ Time _____

Score - W D L _____ 1st/2nd period score _____ /_____ Home☐ Away☐

Position _____   Mood before match: ☺ 😐 ☹

Match was: Very easy☐   Easy☐   Average☐   Hard☐   Very hard☐

Evaluation of my:

   - warm up _____

_____

   - effort and work rate level _____

_____

_____

   - speed _____

   - spacing _____

_____

   - decision making with the ball under pressure_____

_____

_____

Good parts of my play were _____

_____

_____

_____

What I could do better _____

_____

_____

I rate my performance today as_____

What I want to improve upon in practice _____

_____

_____

GAME DAY

Date _____   Tournament ☐

Against _____ Time _____

Score - W D L _____   1st/2nd period score _____ /_____ Home☐ Away☐

Position _____   Mood before match: 😊 😐 ☹️

Match was: Very easy☐   Easy☐   Average☐   Hard☐   Very hard☐

Evaluation of my:

  - warm up _____

_____

  - effort and work rate level _____

_____

_____

  - speed _____

  - spacing _____

_____

  - decision making with the ball under pressure_____

_____

_____

Good parts of my play were _____

_____

_____

_____

What I could do better _____

_____

_____

I rate my performance today as_____

What I want to improve upon in practice _____

_____

_____

GAME DAY

Date _____   Tournament ☐

Against _____ Time _____

Score - W D L _____ 1st/2nd period score _____ /_____ Home☐ Away☐

Position _____   Mood before match: ☺ ☻ ☹

Match was: Very easy☐   Easy☐   Average☐   Hard☐   Very hard☐

Evaluation of my:

- warm up _____

_____

- effort and work rate level _____

_____

_____

- speed _____

- spacing _____

_____

- decision making with the ball under pressure_____

_____

_____

Good parts of my play were _____

_____

_____

_____

What I could do better _____

_____

_____

I rate my performance today as_____

What I want to improve upon in practice _____

_____

GAME DAY

Date _____   Tournament ☐

Against _____ Time _____

Score - W D L _____ 1st/2nd period score _____ /_____ Home ☐ Away ☐

Position _____   Mood before match: ☺ 😐 ☹

Match was: Very easy ☐   Easy ☐   Average ☐   Hard ☐   Very hard ☐

Evaluation of my:

- warm up _____

_____

- effort and work rate level _____

_____

_____

- speed _____

- spacing _____

_____

- decision making with the ball under pressure _____

_____

_____

Good parts of my play were _____

_____

_____

What I could do better _____

_____

_____

I rate my performance today as_____

What I want to improve upon in practice _____

_____

_____

GAME DAY

Date _____ Tournament ☐

Against _____ Time _____

Score - W D L _____ 1st/2nd period score _____ /_____ Home ☐ Away ☐

Position _____ Mood before match: ☺ ☺ ☹

Match was: Very easy ☐ Easy ☐ Average ☐ Hard ☐ Very hard ☐

Evaluation of my:

    - warm up _____

_____

    - effort and work rate level _____

_____

_____

    - speed _____

    - spacing _____

_____

    - decision making with the ball under pressure_____

_____

_____

Good parts of my play were _____

_____

_____

What I could do better _____

_____

_____

I rate my performance today as_____

What I want to improve upon in practice _____

_____

_____

GAME DAY

Date _____

Tournament ☐

Against _____ Time _____

Score - W D L _____ 1st/2nd period score _____ /_____ Home ☐ Away ☐

Position _____ Mood before match: ☺ 😐 ☹

Match was: Very easy ☐ Easy ☐ Average ☐ Hard ☐ Very hard ☐

Evaluation of my:

- warm up _____

_____

- effort and work rate level _____

_____

_____

- speed _____

- spacing _____

_____

- decision making with the ball under pressure_____

_____

_____

Good parts of my play were _____

_____

_____

_____

What I could do better _____

_____

_____

I rate my performance today as_____

What I want to improve upon in practice _____

_____

_____

GAME DAY

Date _____   Tournament ☐

Against _____ Time _____

Score - W D L _____   1st/2nd period score _____ /_____ Home ☐ Away ☐

Position _____ Mood before match: ☺ 😐 ☹

Match was: Very easy ☐   Easy ☐   Average ☐   Hard ☐   Very hard ☐

Evaluation of my:

- warm up _____

_____

- effort and work rate level _____

_____

_____

- speed _____

- spacing _____

_____

- decision making with the ball under pressure_____

_____

_____

Good parts of my play were _____

_____

_____

_____

What I could do better _____

_____

_____

I rate my performance today as_____

What I want to improve upon in practice _____

_____

_____

GAME DAY

Date _____ Tournament ☐

Against _____ Time _____

Score - W D L _____ 1st/2nd period score _____ /_____ Home☐ Away☐

Position _____ Mood before match: 🙂 😐 🙁

Match was: Very easy☐ Easy☐ Average☐ Hard☐ Very hard☐

Evaluation of my:

- warm up _____

_____

- effort and work rate level _____

_____

_____

- speed _____
- spacing _____

_____

- decision making with the ball under pressure_____

_____

_____

Good parts of my play were _____

_____

_____

What I could do better _____

_____

_____

I rate my performance today as_____

What I want to improve upon in practice _____

_____

_____

GAME DAY

Date _____ Tournament ☐

Against _____ Time _____

Score - W D L _____ 1st/2nd period score _____ /_____ Home☐ Away☐

Position _____ Mood before match: 😊 😐 🙁

Match was: Very easy☐   Easy☐   Average☐   Hard☐   Very hard☐

Evaluation of my:

- warm up _____

_____

- effort and work rate level _____

_____

- speed _____

- spacing _____

_____

- decision making with the ball under pressure_____

_____

_____

Good parts of my play were _____

_____

_____

_____

What I could do better _____

_____

_____

I rate my performance today as_____

What I want to improve upon in practice _____

_____

PRACTICE

From Monday _____ to < Friday _____ How many times ___
Date   next game _____ How many times ___
                        Date   Date

1st practice was: Very easy ☐ Easy ☐ Average ☐ Hard ☐ Very hard ☐
2nd practice was: Very easy ☐ Easy ☐ Average ☐ Hard ☐ Very hard ☐
3rd practice was: Very easy ☐ Easy ☐ Average ☐ Hard ☐ Very hard ☐

1st practice: 😊 😐 ☹   2nd practice: 😊 😐 ☹   3rd practice: 😊 😐 ☹

Coach focused on
_____
_____
_____
_____

I focused on
_____
_____
_____
_____

What I'v learnt
_____
_____
_____

My weaknesses/strengths
_____
_____
_____

Coach advice
_____
_____
_____

Additional notes
_____
_____

GAME DAY

Date _____   Tournament ☐

Against _____ Time _____

Score - W D L _____   1st/2nd period score _____ /_____ Home☐ Away☐

Position _____   Mood before match: ☺ ☺ ☹

Match was: Very easy☐   Easy☐   Average☐   Hard☐   Very hard☐

Evaluation of my:

   - warm up _____

_____

   - effort and work rate level _____

_____

_____

   - speed _____
   - spacing _____

_____

   - decision making with the ball under pressure_____

_____

_____

Good parts of my play were _____

_____

_____

_____

What I could do better _____

_____

_____

I rate my performance today as_____

What I want to improve upon in practice _____

_____

_____

GAME DAY

Date _____

Tournament ☐

Against _____ Time _____

Score - W D L _____ 1st/2nd period score _____ / _____ Home ☐ Away ☐

Position _____ Mood before match: ☺ ☺ ☹

Match was: Very easy ☐ Easy ☐ Average ☐ Hard ☐ Very hard ☐

Evaluation of my:

- warm up _____

_____

- effort and work rate level _____

_____

_____

- speed _____

- spacing _____

_____

- decision making with the ball under pressure_____

_____

_____

Good parts of my play were _____

_____

_____

What I could do better _____

_____

_____

I rate my performance today as_____

What I want to improve upon in practice _____

_____

_____

GAME DAY

Date _____ Tournament ☐

Against _____ Time _____

Score - W D L _____ 1st/2nd period score _____ /_____ Home☐ Away☐

Position _____ Mood before match: ☺ 😐 ☹

Match was: Very easy☐   Easy☐   Average☐   Hard☐   Very hard☐

Evaluation of my:

- warm up _____

_____

- effort and work rate level _____

_____

_____

- speed _____

- spacing _____

_____

- decision making with the ball under pressure_____

_____

_____

Good parts of my play were _____

_____

_____

_____

What I could do better _____

_____

_____

I rate my performance today as_____

What I want to improve upon in practice _____

_____

_____

GAME DAY

Date _____ **GAME DAY** Tournament ☐

Against _____ Time _____

Score - W D L _____ 1st/2nd period score _____ /_____ Home☐ Away☐

Position _____ Mood before match: ☺ 😐 ☹

Match was: Very easy☐ Easy☐ Average☐ Hard☐ Very hard☐

Evaluation of my:

- warm up _____

_____

- effort and work rate level _____

_____

_____

- speed _____

- spacing _____

_____

- decision making with the ball under pressure_____

_____

_____

Good parts of my play were _____

_____

_____

What I could do better _____

_____

_____

I rate my performance today as_____

What I want to improve upon in practice _____

_____

_____

GAME DAY

Date _____ Tournament ☐

Against _____ Time _____

Score - W D L _____ 1st/2nd period score _____ / _____ Home ☐ Away ☐

Position _____ Mood before match: ☺ 😐 ☹

Match was: Very easy ☐ Easy ☐ Average ☐ Hard ☐ Very hard ☐

Evaluation of my:

- warm up _____

_____

- effort and work rate level _____

_____

_____

- speed _____

- spacing _____

_____

- decision making with the ball under pressure_____

_____

_____

Good parts of my play were _____

_____

_____

_____

What I could do better _____

_____

_____

I rate my performance today as_____

What I want to improve upon in practice _____

_____

_____